UNDERSTANDING IMMIGRATION

Immigration and the Law

Iris Teichmann

FRANKLIN WATTS
LONDON•SYDNEY

First published in 2005 by Franklin Watts
96 Leonard Street, London EC2A 4XD

Franklin Watts Australia
Level 17/207 Kent Street
Sydney NSW 2000

Series editor: Rachel Cooke
Series Design: Simon Borrough
Picture research: Diana Morris

Dewey Classification: 342.082
A CIP catalogue record for this book is
available from the British Library.

ISBN: 0 7496 6109 7

Printed in Malaysia

Acknowledgements: The author and publishers
would like to thank all those people who were
interviewed for this book. In addition, we would also
like to acknowledge the following sources:
Ng Yuk's story, p.11, National Asian American
Telecommunications Association, *Separate Lives Broken
Dreams*; Hessy's story, p.12, United States Holocaust
Memorial Museum, Washington, D.C.; Paul's story,
p.13, Ellis Island Oral History Collection, interview by
Paul Sigrist, 6/2/1991, recorded at the Ellis Island
recording studio; A Jewish woman's story, p.14, *Daily
Express*, "Six years of waiting without hope",
29/11/1929; Mrs Freer's story, p.15, Museum of
Australia and Ryebuck Media Pty Ltd 2001; US
migrations statistics, p.15, US Bureau of the Census,
9/3/1999; Sham's story, p.16, BBC website,
Immigration and Emigration, "Uganda's loss, Britain's
gain"; migration statistics, p.19, International
Organisation for Migration, World Migration 2003;
population statistics, p.19, United Nations; A
Ukrainian story, p.21, Stepan Shakhno and Cathelijne
Pool, "Reverse effects of restrictive immigration policy
– Ukrainian migrants in the Netherlands"; Sajjad
Saeed's story, p.24, Human Rights Watch, "France:
Towards a just and humane asylum policy", Vol 9,
No 12, October 1997; Hidaya's story, p.25, Dr Gily
Coene, "Gendered Borders", International Conference
on Women and Immigration Law in Europe,
Amsterdam, 30/9/2004 to 2/10/2004, paper for
Workshop on gender, violence and immigration law;
Holta's story, p.26, Save the Children and Salisbury
WORLD, *Home from Home*, page 113; Faezeh's story,
p.27, Amnesty International Australia, "Love and
Suffering", Amnesty Australia on-line, Vol 22 No 7,
February/March 2004; the Melkymian family's story,
p.28, Liz Fekete, *The Deportation Machine*, The
Institute of Race Relations; Ali's story, p.29, British
Refugee Council; A Colombian refugee's story, p.31,
FCJ Hamilton House Refugee Project; Conor's story,
p.32, BBC News on-line, 2/2/2005; Prasob's story,
p.33, *Asian Labour News*, 16/8/2004; Rodolfo's story,
p.37, *The Orlando Sentinel*, "Immigration backlash
worries illegal workers", Sandra Pedicini, 1/6/2002;
Ayaan's story, p.39, Ministerie van Justitie Immigratie
en Naturalisatiedienst, www.ind.nl; population
statistics, p.40, United Nations, *World Population
Prospects – The 2000 Revision*; OECD On-line
Database, www.oecd.org, May 2002, calculations by
the Humboldt University Berlin; Mehdi's story, p.41
Vereniging Vluchtelingen Werk Fryslân, 10/2/2004.

Photographic credits: Bas Fotografie: p.41. Jerry
Bergman/Rex Features: p.12. C Boretz/Image
Works/Topham: p.33. British Library/AKG Images:
p.10b. Mark Chilvers/Panos Pictures: p.20. Paul
Cooper/Rex Features: front cover t, p.29. Matias
Costa/Panos Pictures: p.26. H. Davies/Exile Images:
pp.25, 40. Lou Dematteis/Image Works/Topham: p.30.
J Etchart/Exile Images: p.36. Jeff Greenberg/Image
Works/Topham: p.34. B.Heger/Exile Images: pp.23, 31.
Ute Klaphake/Photofusion: front cover b, pp. 2, 3, 4,
45, 46, 47. Martina Kubaniova: p.35. Piotr
Malecki/Panos Pictures: p. 38. Juana Martinez: p.17.
National Archives and Records Administration –
Pacific Region (San Francisco): p.11. Heldur
Netocny/Panos Pictures: p.22b. North Wind Picture
Archive: p.10t. PA Photos/Empics: p.39. Tess Peni/Rex
Features: p.27. Picturepoint/Topham: p.14. Popperfoto:
p.16. Tina Puryear: p. 18. Rex Features: pp.9, 21.
Roger-Viollet/Topham: pp.13, 15. Tony Savino/Image
Works/Topham: p.37. Trygve Sorvaag/Panos Pictures:
p.24. Dermot Tatlow/Panos Pictures: p.8. Horst
Teichmann: p.22t. Topham: pp.19, 32. Sven
Torfinn/Panos Pictures: p.28.

Contents

Explaining immigration laws

Immigration control

Every year millions of people around the world attempt to move from one country to another; to seek a better life, to improve their career and work prospects, or to find safety from war or human rights abuses. However, no one can legally immigrate to another country without the permission of that country's government. Every country has immigration laws that the authorities use to decide when, under what conditions and for how long a person can enter and stay.

This Mongolian police officer is taking down a driver's details before allowing him across the border from China.

Immigration status

Immigration laws set out the legal status of immigrants in their new home. Different types of immigration status may be granted, each with different rights and conditions. A business visa, for example, allows a person to remain in a country for a limited period. The person is only allowed to carry out the business specified in the visa and cannot take up any other work. A settlement visa allows a person to live and work freely in another country for good.

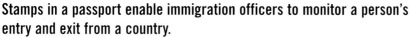

Stamps in a passport enable immigration officers to monitor a person's entry and exit from a country.

Controlling exit

Some developing and less developed countries also control emigration. This means that their citizens need permission from their government to leave the country. This is because developing countries do not wish to lose skilled workers who may seek better conditions elsewhere. Developed countries are more concerned about controlling who can enter, rather than who can leave.

Global impact

During the 19th and early 20th centuries, growing countries such as Australia, the USA and Canada welcomed immigrants in huge numbers and encouraged people to settle. Today, the governments of these countries seek not only to restrict the number of immigrants, but also to select the type of people who are allowed in. For these countries and for many in Europe, immigration is a big issue, as people from less developed countries seek entry, both legally and illegally.

AS A MATTER OF FACT

Emigration: Leaving one's home country permanently. People going from their country to live somewhere else are called emigrants.

Immigration: Arriving in another country in order to work and live there. Usually, people have to ask for permission to enter their adopted country before they travel. People who come to a country to live and work permanently are called immigrants. Migrants are people who come to work and live in another country temporarily.

Passport: A document issued by the government of a country to identify the holder as a citizen of that nation and to give the person permission to travel abroad and return home again.

Visa: An entry made in a passport by a government official that gives the passport holder permission to enter that government's country.

9

Immigration control in the past

Chinese workers building a railway in the USA in the 1860s. Migrants often made up the workforce on large-scale projects like this.

The price of entry

Until the late 19th century, immigration to the developed countries of the world was relatively easy. Immigrants were mostly tolerated, especially if they brought valuable skills and wealth to their adopted country. Would-be immigrants could, however, be denied entry if they were thought to be competing with native workers or had insufficient funds to support themselves. Even after they were established, immigrant communities could be expelled from a country on religious grounds.

A JEWISH STORY: NO CHOICES

In 1492, King Ferdinand of Spain expelled all Jewish people from the kingdom to ensure the dominance of the Catholic faith. Four years later, King Manuel of Portugal, another Catholic monarch, thought about doing the same. However, at the last minute, he changed his mind as he did not want to lose the Portuguese Jews' skills and economic talents. Instead, he closed Portugal's ports and gave the Jewish population 20 years to adopt Christian beliefs. Most Jews complied, but some preferred suicide rather than give up their faith.

A service at a synaogue in Spain in about 1350. The Jews came to Spain in the 2nd century CE when they were expelled from Israel by the Romans.

Excluding Asian immigrants

The vast majority of people who moved to countries such as the USA, Australia and Canada in the 19th and early 20th centuries came from Europe. However, an increasing number of Asians, mostly from China, travelled to the USA and Australia to find work in these countries' rapidly expanding industries.

The United States was the first country to pass a law intended to stop further immigration from Asia and to ensure that local workers did not have to compete with Asians for jobs. The 1882 Chinese Exclusion Act made it very difficult for new Chinese arrivals to set foot in the country as only those who had the skills to work and contribute to the economy were admitted. Australia followed the USA by passing the Immigration Restriction Act of 1901, in response to local resistance towards Asian immigration.

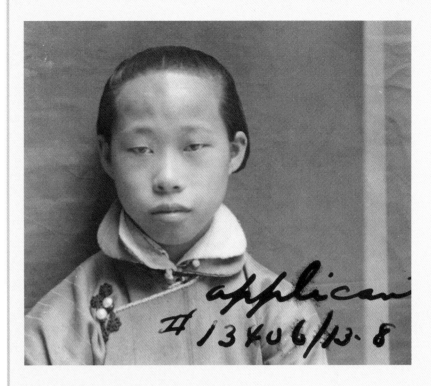

NG YUK'S STORY: CONVINCING THE IMMIGRATION OFFICIALS

Ng Yuk (shown above) was a 20-year-old Chinese woman who immigrated to the USA in 1914. Her 37-year-old husband was already a US citizen. On her arrival both she and her husband were interviewed by an immigration official. They had to give details about their wedding and their life together in Hong Kong. Although their stories differed slightly, in the end the immigration official allowed Ng Yuk into the country.

One of the reasons why the US authorities were reluctant to admit Chinese women was because many of them were forced by their husbands into prostitution on arrival in the USA. It seems that Ng Yuk suffered just such a fate – she wrote to an immigration office saying she was **"sold into slavery [prostitution]"**. Her letter continued:

"I wish to ask you to rescue me and send me back to China, and I will thank you thousands of times for it."

It seems likely that Ng Yuk got her wish and was deported back to China.

Monitoring arrivals

The 20th century saw developed countries begin to place more restrictions on immigration in an attempt to control the numbers of new arrivals. Governments of these countries began to demand that prospective immigrants apply to their embassies abroad for permission to enter. Immigration officials would look for visa stamps in passports and other identity documents to see whether immigrants had the required legal permission to enter the country. It became very difficult to be allowed in without a visa.

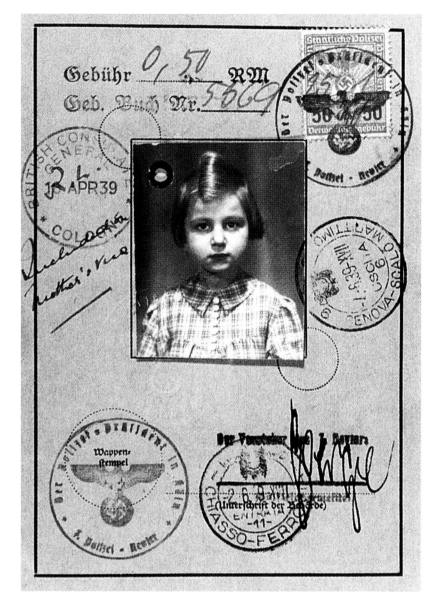

An identity document of a Jewish girl issued by the Nazi German authorities in the 1930s.

HESSY'S STORY: TRYING TO GET A VISA

Hessy Levinson Taft was born in 1934 in Germany. She describes her father's attempt to obtain visas for the family to emigrate from France to the USA:

"An American immigration visa is hard to get, because you need to prove that you can sustain yourself and you're not going to land up being on welfare or a burden to anyone in the country ... and that you are in good health. But even after all this, you are told that you have 90 days to reach American shores. And my father realised as time was going by that there was no way in which he could get his family to the US within the time frame left. Thirty days before the visa expired, he requested an extension from Washington. The Atlantic, you know, across the Atlantic, there were no commercial flights at the time. This was in 1941. The ocean was patrolled. We waited for a reply from Washington. And [it] eventually came, and it said, 'no'."

In the end, the Cuban consulate in Nice, France, gave Hessy and her family a visa to immigrate to Cuba.

Enforcing immigration laws

Introducing immigration laws meant appointing officials who would control ports and borders and enforce those laws. At the end of the 19th century, the USA became the first country to set up a separate immigration authority. Immigration officials were stationed at border points and key ports of entry to screen and monitor arrivals. Other countries followed suit, although European countries only really started to increase their reliance on immigration officials when the number of immigrants rose after the Second World War (1939–45).

Screening arrivals

From the late 19th century, the most famous entry point into the USA was the immigration station on Ellis Island in New York, which opened on 2 January 1892. There, newly arrived immigrants were interviewed and allowed into the country if they had money or family members already in the country. Otherwise they were detained.

New arrivals at Ellis Island in about 1900.

PAUL'S STORY: DETAINED AT ELLIS ISLAND

Paul Laric was 14 when he came to the USA from Yugoslavia via India. He and his family were detained at Ellis Island on arrival in 1940. He describes what it was like:

"The place was filled. There were people in similar circumstances who had their papers looked at and reprocessed. There were others who had been there for weeks and some for months, some as much as a year. And there was a feeling of desperation because we had no idea when we would get out and neither did the other people. The other feeling was that, this being wartime and the influx of immigrants at such a high level, it was understandable that the United States would be very careful in screening the people that it admitted. And so there was a great deal of suspicion as to who was being admitted, and for that reason also there was a feeling of privacy that we wanted to observe and not mingle with the other detainees because we had no idea who they were."

13

Not wanted

Restricting immigration was not simply a response to the increasing numbers of people seeking entry. The industrialising countries also used immigration laws, such as the Chinese Exclusion Act in the USA, to prohibit the immigration of people they did not want. In 1905, Britain passed the Aliens Act, which allowed the government to refuse entry to people who were ill, thought likely to become a burden on society or simply not wanted. The act was used to keep out many Jewish people who were fleeing persecution across Europe.

Nationality quotas

Despite the restrictions, many Europeans continued to emigrate, most of them trying to get into the USA. Immigration to Europe and Australia, however, remained low. The US government grew concerned about the impact of immigration and imposed a nationality quota system in the 1920s – the only country to do so. This meant that a set number of immigrants from each country were allowed in annually. For those people still intent on going to the USA, this could mean a long wait if quotas had already been filled.

A JEWISH WOMAN'S STORY: STUCK IN TRANSIT

In the 1920s, many would-be Jewish immigrants who were en route to the USA were stranded in a hostel in Southampton, England. They could not travel further because of the USA's newly imposed quotas on the numbers of immigrants from different nationalities. An English newspaper interviewed a Jewish woman, aged 60, who was waiting for a visa to join her children in the USA:

"The children write to me from New York and say, 'You must come to us soon', and I write back saying, 'I think I shall never come before I am dead.' They cannot understand that six years of waiting here has broken my spirit. Whose fault it is that we have been waiting for six years I do not know. I am now number 15 on the quota list, but that does not mean that I go soon to New York. It may mean many more years of waiting yet."

German Jewish refugees arrive in Southampton.

AS A MATTER OF FACT

Between 1850 and 1930 immigration to the USA increased from approximately 2.2 million people to 14.2 million each year. Throughout this period more than 95 per cent of these people came from Europe.

All immigrants who arrived in the USA were given a health check before being allowed entry.

Choosing carefully

Although the USA, Britain and Australia had passed laws to restrict immigration they were, at times, prepared to ignore those laws. Faced by acute labour shortages, they accepted large numbers of immigrants who had arrived without visas and, strictly speaking, were attempting entry illegally. It was mainly those immigrants who were fit and strong enough to work who were allowed in. Immigrants could also be granted, or refused, entry on moral grounds.

MRS FREER'S STORY: NOT WANTED

In 1936, Mrs Freer, an English woman, had left her husband in South Africa for another man. When she and her new partner attempted to come to Australia, Mrs Freer was tested in Italian (a language she did not speak) to make sure she failed the entry test into Australia. The Australian authorities did not want her in the country because they considered her behaviour immoral. They exploited their immigration laws to ensure she did not gain entry.

15

Immigration control today

Non-European immigration

During the 1960s, the countries to which people traditionally immigrated as well as European nations began to see a rise in non-European immigrants. Some of the local population in developed countries saw these newcomers as a threat to their own way of life. As a result, developed countries began to pass further immigration laws to restrict immigration from the developing world. Events such as the arrival in the UK of 27,000 Ugandan Asians in 1970s became the exception rather than the rule.

A family, newly arrived from Uganda, have their first meal in Britain.

SHAM KARNIK'S STORY: BENDING THE RULES

In 1972, the president and dictator of Uganda, Idi Amin, expelled all Asians living in the country. Britain, which had once run Uganda as a colony, relaxed its laws restricting immigration to allow Ugandan Asians into the UK. The Ugandan Asian Sham Karnik and his family were housed in a camp on arrival in the UK, but a local man offered them a room:

"Neela [his wife], my two young daughters and my sister and I took the room, and made a start in a new life. I was quickly back to work, signing on at the Labour Exchange, the forerunner of today's Job Centre, and started work at the Guardian Royal Exchange within two weeks."

Like Sham, many of the Ugandan Asians who arrived in 1972 have built very successful careers and businesses.

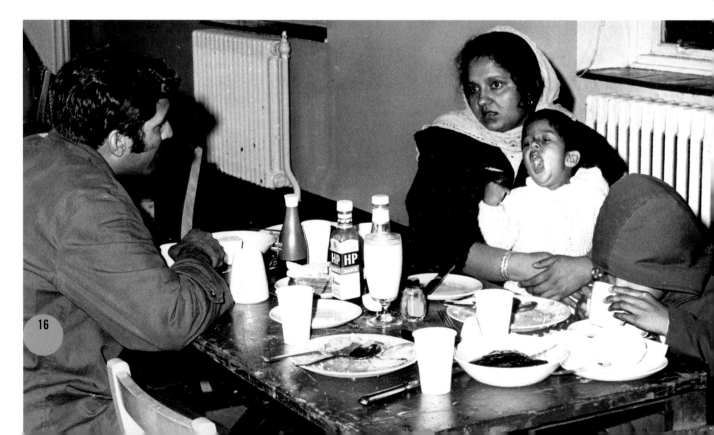

Reuniting families

Being able to be with your family is recognised by most governments as a basic human right. Today, one of the few ways of applying to live in another country legally is to apply to join a close family member who is already a permanent resident in the country. Most developed countries offer family reunion visas because they believe that immigrants adapt better to their new life when they have the support and help of their immediate family. This means that they are unlikely to have to fall back on government help.

Marriage visas

Another way to be allowed to live in another country permanently is to marry a citizen of that country. It is not unusual for a person to arrive on a temporary visa, get married and then apply to stay in the country permanently. Governments want to avoid marriage being an easy route to legal settlement and so a very strict test is applied before the application to stay is granted. Each partner is usually interviewed separately and marriage registrars will tell the immigration authorities if they suspect that a couple is marrying simply for immigration reasons.

JUANA'S STORY: FROM NICARAGUA TO AUSTRALIA

Juana is from Managua, the capital of Nicaragua. She met her Australian husband, Alan, when they worked together at the Ministry of Foreign Affairs in the mid 1980s. Their two children were born in Nicaragua, but before they reached school age the family decided to move back to Australia. Juana feels she's been lucky:

"Nowadays, it's very difficult to get a visa to settle in Australia. When I applied to join my husband, the process was very straightforward and I got a visa very quickly for the children and myself. A friend of mine applied recently to stay in Australia, but the authorities didn't believe her and her husband were really together, even though she was expecting his child at the time. By the time she got her visa, their child was nearly a year old."

Juana (right) with her family on holiday in Finland. She and Alan had a third child after settling in Australia.

17

Work visas

Developed countries have set up different legal immigration routes for potential migrants. Many people move abroad for work, for example. Countries may allow people to come and work on a temporary basis by granting a business visa or a work visa, for which the migrant has to apply before arrival. To obtain a work visa, applicants normally need to be sponsored by an employer in the country to which they wish to move. If, at some future date, they wish to change employers, they have to reapply for another work visa.

TINA'S STORY: A NEW WORKING LIFE

In 2001, Tina left her native North Carolina, USA to take up a job in London. She initially came on a student visa, which allowed her to work a limited number of hours a week. She then applied for a job that she had seen advertised in a British newspaper. When she was appointed, the employer helped her obtain a work permit so she could work full time.

"I applied for a post at a UK charity when I arrived in the country. I was offered the job after attending an interview. I was competing against British jobseekers who applied for the post as well. Therefore, in order to get the work permit from the British authorities, my prospective employer had to show that they had taken all steps to advertise the job widely and prove I was the best candidate for the job. I guess they hired me because I had already gained considerable, valuable experience in the field back home that others didn't have."

Today, Tina continues to work in Britain. Her work permit was granted for seven years. If she wants to continue working in the UK after her work permit expires, either in the same post or a new one, she will have to apply for a new work permit.

From temporary to permanent status

Many European countries will allow a person to stay indefinitely if a work visa has been renewed several times. This is usually because governments recognise that the person has established roots in the country and has contributed taxes for some time. In such a situation, it would be unreasonable to deny the person permanent residence.

Grape pickers at work during harvest time in France – a time when vineyards need to recruit extra workers.

Working for a season

Many developed countries have huge agricultural industries that rely heavily on a supply of low-skilled workers who are prepared to work on a seasonal basis. To fill this need, governments grant temporary work visas to foreign migrants. A seasonal work visa usually allows the person to work for one particular employer for a few months. If the migrants want to come back the next year, he or she has to apply for a new work visa. As temporary residents, people who come to a country to work on a seasonal basis cannot stay indefinitely, even though they may return year after year.

AS A MATTER OF FACT

Immigrant admissions to the USA, Canada, Australia and New Zealand in 2000:

	USA	Canada	Australia	New Zealand
Family-sponsored	584,159	60,517	33,470	26,701
Employment-based	107,024	132,118	44,730	18,096
Humanitarian-based and refugees	125,024	60,060	21,770	5,212
Asylum seekers	6,858	-	5,740	-
Total immigrants	823,035	192,178	105,710	50,009
Overall population:	285 million	31 million	19 million	3.8 million

Asylum seekers: People applying to be recognised as refugees (see pages 24–25).

Employment-based: Immigration status given to people coming to work in a country.

Family-sponsored: Immigration status granted when a person joins close family members in another country. They usually have to show that their family members already resident can support them.

Humanitarian: An often temporary immigration status, usually granted to people fleeing civil war or other dangerous situations in their country.

Refugees: People who have fled persecution in their country. Refugee status is recognised under international law (see pages 22–23).

The European Union

In today's global economy it is generally easy for businesses to move money and assets around the world. By contrast, the movement of workers is restricted by immigration laws. However, the European Union (EU) tries to combine free trade with freedom of movement.

The EU has its origins in 1951, when Belgium, the Netherlands, Luxembourg, Italy, France and West Germany set up a free trade area for the steel and coal industries – the European Coal and Steel Community. In 1957, this was effectively expanded by the Treaty of Rome to form the European Economic Community, or Common Market. Member countries allowed the free and unrestricted movement of goods, people and capital within their territories. Denmark, Ireland and the United Kingdom joined in 1973, followed by Greece in 1981, Spain and Portugal in 1986 and Austria, Finland and Sweden in 1995. The European Economic Community became the European Union in 1992.

A common market

The EU is mainly about free trade. This means that member countries can import and export goods freely amongst themselves, thus keeping costs down. It also means that EU member countries agree on what tariffs they impose on non-EU countries for selling goods to them. A national of an EU member country is also a citizen of the European Union. This means that they can move to and live in any other EU country, and vote and stand in elections for the European parliament. EU citizenship does not replace national citizenship, but is an additional status.

Being able to move and work freely in other EU countries means that EU citizens have become a very mobile workforce, pursuing career and business opportunities across Europe.

EU expansion

On 1 May 2004, the EU was greatly expanded by the addition of the Czech Republic, Cyprus, Estonia, Latvia, Lithuania, Hungary, Malta, Poland, the Slovak Republic and Slovenia. Citizens of these countries can now travel freely to any other EU country, but the new members will have to wait a number of years before they are permitted to work in the existing EU countries. This is because some fear that too many people might come seeking jobs. Many more countries, such as Ukraine and Turkey, want to join the EU. However, for their citizens the possibility of becoming an EU national and therefore being able to live and work freely across the EU is still a long way off.

A UKRAINIAN'S STORY: STAYING ON

Like many others from Ukraine, this female migrant worker went to the Netherlands on a temporary work visa. She overstayed her visit as it would have been too difficult to renew her temporary visa:

"The most important things are connections and valid documentation. Then you feel as a human not as a slave. I stayed for a year with my month visa. I had to be extremely cautious, especially while going shopping in daytime, not to be caught red-handed with no valid documentation. I also worked night hours mainly, because I had to commute to my work place and wished to avoid the police."

An unpoliced border crossing between Denmark and Germany, both EU members.

Asylum laws

HORST'S STORY: ASYLUM FROM COMMUNISM

Born in 1934, Horst was living in what became East Germay after the Second World War. In this Cold War era, he decided to flee secretly to West Germany, without telling even his parents. He managed to get to West Berlin in 1964, three years after the Soviets had built the Berlin Wall dividing East and West Berlin:

"When I got to the emergency reception centre in West Berlin, the British, American and Soviet authorities all interviewed me about my reasons for leaving communist East Germany. I then had to attend a hearing with a panel of seven officials who decided that I could stay in West Germany. They wanted to know in what way I had actually supported the communist regime. In the end, they decided that I could stay."

Protecting refugees

The Second World War resulted in millions of people being displaced from their homes. This refugee crisis led to the development of laws that would guarantee basic human rights to citizens and make governments responsible for protecting people fleeing persecution. In 1951, many countries signed the Refugee Convention, agreeing to be responsible for protecting people who have fled persecution by granting them asylum.

An Afghan refugee who has fled to Pakistan.

AS A MATTER OF FACT: THE DEVELOPMENT OF HUMAN RIGHTS

The Refugee Convention is based on the recognition by the international community that situations will always arise that cause people to flee their homes. The right to seek asylum was enshrined in the 1948 Universal Declaration of Human Rights, which among other things requires governments around the world to guarantee their citizens basic rights, including the right to life, freedom, shelter and education. Unlike the Refugee Convention it does not have the force of law, but it underpins all the international laws that United Nations member countries are pledged to uphold.

Defining refugees

The Refugee Convention defines a "refugee" as someone who has left their country and fears persecution if they returned because of their race, nationality, sex, religion or political opinion. The refugee definition is important because it not only allows governments to decide whether or not someone is a refugee, but also means they can give recognised refugees a proper immigration status. Otherwise refugees would have no status and therefore no rights in the new country. The traditional immigration countries – Australia, Canada and the USA – have for decades allowed refugees in such situations to apply to be resettled there.

Life without status

Not all countries have signed the Refugee Convention and therefore do not protect refugees by giving them immigration status. Pakistan, for example, has not signed the convention but nonetheless tolerates the presence of over a million refugees, many of whom have fled neighbouring Afghanistan. These refugees have no rights in Pakistan because they have not officially been granted permission to stay in the country.

A Colombian refugee applying for asylum in Ecuador with the help of a member of the Office of the United Nations High Commissioner for Refugees (UNHCR).

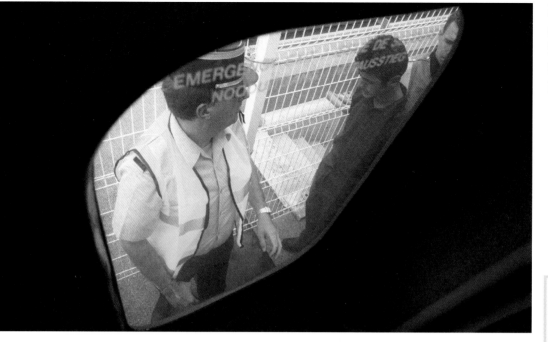

French police arrest someone trying to cross to the UK on a Eurostar train.

Seeking asylum

Another term for being recognised as a refugee is being granted asylum. Asylum usually refers to people who are given refugee status after they have arrived in a new country. People applying for asylum are called asylum seekers, and different governments have passed their own domestic asylum laws setting out the formal procedures for dealing with them.

These laws describe what the asylum process is and under what circumstances people can apply for asylum. They say what rights and support asylum seekers may have while they wait for a decision, how long that decision is likely to take, and what happens if their asylum application is successful or if it is refused. But many countries make it very difficult for people even to gain access to the asylum process.

SAJJAD SAEED'S STORY: IN TRANSIT IN FRANCE

In 1996, Sajjad Saeed, who comes from Pakistan, tried to apply for asylum in Britain. Because he had travelled via France, the UK authorities sent him back there to pursue his asylum claim. Even though a refugee charity in London had contacted border police in Calais, France, to tell them that Sajjad wanted to apply for asylum, the French authorities immediately put him in custody and prepared to deport him. But the Pakistani embassy refused to issue him with an identity document and the French authorities could not send him back to Pakistan. Sajjad's current whereabouts are unknown.

The asylum process

Once a person has been allowed to apply for asylum, the authorities will interview the applicant and examine the human rights situation in his or her home country and any evidence the applicant can put forward to back up his or her fears of returning home. Applicants have to show that the government in their home country is in fact persecuting them personally. People fleeing from a war zone, but not directly targeted by their government, are unlikely to be accepted. Applicants can usually appeal against an initial negative decision.

Making a case

Asylum seekers often depend on the ability of a specialist lawyer to make a good case on their behalf. Many who are rejected the first time round are successful on appeal. If governments find that an asylum seeker does not meet the requirements for refugee status but feel that the situation in his or her country is quite dangerous, perhaps because of political instability or civil war, they may grant temporary asylum on humanitarian grounds.

The long fight between different tribal clans in Somalia has caused many Somalis to flee to the West.

HIDAYA'S STORY: REFUSED AT FIRST

Hidaya is from Somalia and applied for asylum in Belgium. Her asylum application was initially rejected because she didn't know that she had to provide as many details about her story as possible.

"They said, 'You did not specify the story in details, you told us the story in general.' I didn't know. They had an interpreter who was just translating for me, and when I was telling the truth and what had happened, he was telling me, 'No, this ... is just about how you arrived in Belgium and why you ran away from Somalia and how long have you been away from Somalia. That's the only [thing] they need from you now...' He was not interested in listening."

Hidaya was interviewed again several times at her appeal. After seven months of waiting she was finally granted asylum in Belgium.

HOLTA'S STORY: ANXIOUS WAIT

Holta is 14 and from Kosovo. He is an asylum seeker in the UK:

"I have been here five years now. I feel very isolated and anxious. There are times when I can't stand it and want the Home Office to make their decision as quickly as possible so that I know what will happen to me for sure and can get on with my life. The waiting is the hardest thing, as you are completely unsure about the future. I feel as if my life depends upon a bit of paper."

A Bangladeshi migrant, held at a refugee centre in Italy, waits for a decision on his request for asylum.

Deterring more arrivals

As the numbers of people applying for asylum in developed countries increased in the 1980s and 1990s, the governments of those countries revised their asylum procedures to try and deter asylum seekers. Measures have included increased immigration checks at airports abroad, intercepting people trying to arrive by boat and not allowing access to the asylum process for people who are thought to have come from safe countries.

Restricting rights

Governments also believe that arrivals can be deterred by restricting rights and support for asylum seekers who are already in the country pursuing an application. Most developed countries have severely restricted the amount of money asylum seekers have to live on, while at the same time not allowing them to find work. Asylum seekers are therefore forced to rely on meagre government handouts while unable to make a living for themselves. The situation is made worse when, as can often happen, the authorities take some time to consider their asylum applications.

FAEZEH'S STORY: KEPT IN ISOLATION

Faezeh and her family fled Iran because of religious troubles. After a dangerous journey by boat, which took 10 days from Java, they arrived at Port Hedland in Australia. They were detained on arrival.

"After two days, the Department of Immigration (DIMIA) came to interview us. I am older than my sister and brothers so I was interviewed separately from the rest of my family. I was very scared and didn't understand the legal system that I had just become part of. I needed some advice but I didn't get any. Seventy-three of us, the people who arrived on the same boat, were kept in isolation for seven months. We were allowed outside for about half an hour in the morning and half an hour in the afternoon.

After we had our first interview with a lawyer and then with a case worker, we could go to the 'free camp'. This meant that we could go buy stuff from the canteen and order stuff. That night I saw the night sky and the stars and the moon, and we could also phone our family and we could see Australian TV, read newspapers and magazines and listen to music."

Faezeh is now engaged to a Palestinian refugee and lives with her family in Sydney. It took several months for them to get a permanent visa.

A refugee detention centre in Australia.

Detention

In order to speed up the deportation of asylum seekers who are unsuccessful with their applications, some countries have also increased the use of detention. More and more governments detain asylum seekers early on in the process if they think the person is unlikely to keep in touch with the authorities. Detention also prevents the asylum seeker from living in and becoming part of a community and so building up a life for themselves. Doing so could make it more difficult for the authorities to deport them later on. Life under detention can be very harsh and many people decide to return home, even if they have a good asylum case.

27

Deportation

Asylum seekers who have been unsuccessful with their applications, and who have exhausted the asylum process's avenues for appeal, are effectively without immigration status until they can be returned to their home countries. Often the immigration authorities are unable to return them, perhaps because their home country refuses to accept them back, or the person is too ill too travel or a separate application for permission to stay is pending.

South African police and immigration officials prepare to deport illegal immigrants back to Zimbabwe.

THE MELKYMIAN FAMILY'S STORY: NO WAY BACK

The Melkymian family has no citizenship but are of Armenian origin. They had applied unsuccessfully for asylum in Sweden. The Swedish immigration authorities tried to deport them to Azerbaijan on a specially chartered flight. The plan failed, however, because the authorities in Baku, Azerbaijan's capital, refused to accept the family and threatened to confiscate the plane if it did not return to Europe.

In limbo

People who are no longer classed as asylum seekers, but are unable to return home, are in a precarious situation. They have no rights to government support, are usually not allowed to work and may end up in limbo for a considerable amount of time. They may sometimes be allowed to work if it becomes clear that they cannot be sent home, but they may be required to report to the authorities on a regular basis. Uncertainty as to their status makes it very difficult for these people to build a proper life.

ALI'S STORY: TRYING TO WORK

Ali is an asylum seeker in the UK. He was allowed to work when he first arrived (the UK has since changed its laws, denying asylum seekers permission to work). Ali had no identity documents, but simply a letter from the immigration authorities stating his name and that he had applied for asylum.

"I thought when I arrived here it would be freedom, or at least liberty compared to other places. I want to fix myself ... [but] with the papers they give you, it's not easy to look for work – the letter has 'you are liable to be detained' on it. The paperwork separates you from the people."

Ali has not been able to find work. He thinks this is because, even though the authorities have allowed him to work, employers immediately see he is an asylum seeker and therefore do not employ him.

Proving one's identity

It has been notoriously difficult for western governments to return some nationals back to their home countries. The Chinese authorities, for example, will not accept people back without proper documentation. Yet most Chinese immigrants travel on false documentation and may have no evidence to show that they are who they claim to be. China also punishes people who have left the country without prior permission, making Chinese immigrants reluctant to go back.

A 16-year-old Kurdish refugee. The number he displays is his only official form of identification.

29

Illegal immigration

Chinese illegal immigrants found on a boat trying to get into the USA.

The smuggling business

To some extent the rise in illegal immigration has come about because western governments now operate such strict immigration controls, not only at the borders of their own countries, but also at airports abroad from which asylum seekers are known to travel. Often the only option for people wanting to get to the West is to rely on illegal, and hazardous, smuggling networks.

AS A MATTER OF FACT

Smuggling is not the same as trafficking. Smugglers help other people – either for free or for money – to obtain false identity and travel documentation in order to travel illegally to another country. The person being smuggled agrees to being transported illegally. Traffickers may initially have someone's consent to take them illegally to another country, but will then seize the person's documents and force them to work against their will when they arrive at their destination.

Both smuggling and trafficking are illegal, but governments have difficulties prosecuting them because people are usually too afraid to speak out against the people who have smuggled or trafficked them.

From illegal immigrant to asylum seeker

The media in the developed world often use the term "asylum seeker" interchangeably with "illegal immigrant", the implication being that all asylum seekers are illegal immigrants. Whether an asylum seeker has entered the country illegally or not does not affect the outcome of an asylum application. People who have entered a country illegally and subsequently apply for asylum have legal status as asylum seekers within the country while the authorities decide on their case.

The realities of refugee flight

For many people in the West it is difficult to understand why people fleeing their home country have to travel illegally. This is because most people fleeing conflict or persecution simply cannot risk approaching the authorities to request a passport. Even if they already possess passports the urgency of the situation may be such that there is not enough time to travel to the nearest embassy – which may be hundreds of kilometres away – to apply for a visa. Travelling illegally on false documentation may be the only option for desperate people.

Many Colombians, like this family, have fled their country because of violence and political unrest. Most end up in neighbouring countries, such as Ecuador.

A COLOMBIAN REFUGEE'S STORY: TRYING THE LEGAL WAY

"I left Colombia because my husband was assassinated and shortly thereafter I started receiving anonymous phone calls. I went into hiding and within a month I fled Bogotá. Five months later [my husbands' enemies] found me again and started a fire in my room. I was very afraid now and in danger, so I decided to get out of Colombia. I decided to go to the US embassy to get a visa. I didn't realize how difficult it would be to get a visa. For a full year I stayed in different places. I was finally able to get a visa to the USA."

Becoming illegal

Illegal immigrants are not necessarily people who have arrived in a country illegally. In fact, a considerable number of people who have entered a country legally may for one reason or another lose their legal status. For example, someone who has arrived on a student or short-term work visa and fails to leave the country at the end of their stay becomes an illegal immigrant. It may simply be that they forgot to extend their visa, or because they were afraid they would not have their stay extended and decided to stay on illegally.

CONOR'S STORY: OVERSTAYING A VISA

Conor is 33 and from Northern Ireland. He went to Australia on a working-holiday visa, which expired in 1997. He then spent two years working illegally by falsely declaring himself a resident on his new tax form and continuing to do agency work and a bar job.

"It's amazing how many people are illegal from the UK and the majority find it easy to get casual work paid cash in hand. The questioning was far from hostile. They gave me a cup of tea and asked me why I overstayed. I told them I had met someone, who is now my wife, and didn't want to go back. They asked me where I worked but never asked for names or addresses."

Even though Conor was banned from entering Australia for three years, he came back after 18 months. He was allowed in because he applied for residency. He is now an Australian citizen.

As in many big cities, Sydney's bars and restaurants offer plenty of opportunities for casual work.

Illegal working

Illegal immigrants usually only become known to the authorities if they work illegally and their employer reports them to the authorities. In order to reduce illegal working, developed countries have laws that make employers responsible for checking that the people they hire have the right documentation and are allowed to work in the country. But some employers are still prepared to take the risk of employing illegal immigrants, who are usually prepared to work for less.

PRASOB'S STORY: DEPORTED UNPAID

Prasob is from Thailand. He worked illegally at a bakery in Auckland, New Zealand, for seven years for an hourly wage of NZ$4.70 – about half the country's minimum wage for adults. He was caught by the immigration authorities and deported back to Thailand without receiving the wages he was owed. Had he been paid on a legal basis, his back pay would have amounted to over NZ$100,000. Prasob is not allowed to return to New Zealand for at least five years. His employer was fined NZ$2,000.

Women working in a "sweat shop" in New York, USA.

The scale of illegal immigration

The numbers of illegal immigrants detected by immigration authorities in developed countries is rising. It is thought that around a third to a half of new arrivals in developed countries enter illegally – about 20 per cent more than in the early 1990s. In the UK, for example, 3,300 illegal immigrants came to the notice of the authorities in 1990. By 2000, this had risen to 47,000. There are an estimated 12 million illegal immigrants in the USA.

33

From immigrant to citizen

Permanent settlement and citizenship are crucial to be able to build and enjoy a new life abroad.

Being a citizen

When we use the word "citizen", we usually mean any person who lives and works in a country legally and pays taxes. But in the context of immigration law, a citizen is defined as a national of a country, or someone who has that country's nationality. Immigrants can only become citizens of a country if they successfully apply for citizenship. Before immigrants can even think about taking on their new country's nationality, they first need to have permanent immigration status.

Staying on

People who are already legally resident in a country, such as those on a work visa, a visitor visa or a student visa, will have to apply to the authorities for an extension to their visa if they wish to stay for longer. But they cannot apply to stay and settle for good on these types of visa. Obtaining a marriage visa, a family reunion visa, a special immigration programme or an asylum application are the only ways to apply to stay in another country for good.

MARTINA'S STORY: STUDY AND WORK

Martina is 30 and from the Slovak Republic. A student agency in Bratislava, Slovakia's capital, helped her find an English school in London, which in turn helped her get a student visa that allowed her to work for a maximum of 20 hours a week. Since her arrival in 2002, Martina has worked in many different jobs and has reduced her expenditure by sharing one room with other students.

"I worked as a live-in carer. Then I was a waitress in a restaurant, but the worst job was delivering leaflets at night in Soho, London's West End. My student visa ran out, but I could only get my visa renewed if I could show that I had enough money in my bank account to support myself. My friends helped me get the money together so I could stay. Then I got the chance to edit a community magazine, which at least gave me a job that matched my level of education. Unfortunately, the magazine folded and now I work as a care assistant again while studying English."

Martina is enjoying her time in London but hopes to go back home eventually.

Settlement

Being able to stay indefinitely in another country, but not necessarily having that country's nationality, is called settlement. Having settlement status means that people can stay as long as they want, have access to government support, can work like any other citizen and do not have to report to the immigration authorities. It can happen in some countries that the immigration authorities will not allow a person with settlement status back into the country if they have been abroad for too long.

From illegal to legal

Illegal immigrants usually find it extremely difficult to gain legal status. Immigration authorities tend to try and deport illegal immigrants back to their country once they have detected them. A person who has had a previously poor immigration history in a country will also find it difficult to get a visa to return to that country. The authorities may fear that the person will try to stay on illegally or apply for asylum when their visa runs out.

35

Acquiring rights

Although illegal immigrants may not obtain visas, they can acquire certain rights. There are many cases of immigrants who have stayed for many years in another country without the knowledge of the authorities. They have built a life for themselves, worked and perhaps even raised a family. In such circumstances, the authorities may allow them to stay for good, as asking them to leave would mean completely uprooting them and their families.

Spanish police officers stop two Arab youths and ask for their identity documents.

Changing status

Sometimes governments grant amnesties to certain groups of migrants. In the USA there are proposals for a law allowing illegal immigrants to apply for a three-year working visa, provided they have got a job. For illegal workers, the law would mean a secure future and access to the same employment rights as other US citizens. For the government, it is an effective way of dealing with illegal immigrants, without businesses losing their workforce. However, many people oppose the plan, saying that migrants should not be rewarded for being in a country illegally.

Having recently arrived in the USA, these Mexicans are working at a car-wash.

RODOLFO'S STORY: WITHOUT STATUS

A 26-year-old migrant worker from Mexico heard about the US government's proposal to allow illegal immigrants to apply for temporary work permits. In an interview with a newspaper, he called himself Rodolfo, but did not want to give his real name for fear of being detected and deported back to Mexico.

"There is fear. You are undocumented, and you cannot ask for your rights. If you are undocumented, you are always lost."

He admits to feeling powerless as he and his co-workers cannot complain about low wages or working conditions. Nor are they willing to risk returning to Mexico to visit their families.

Becoming a citizen

Immigrants who have settlement and have lived in a country for a number of years can usually apply for citizenship. The process of applying for citizenship is also called "naturalisation". A person who has acquired citizenship and has been recognised as a national of his or her adopted country can live and work freely, gain access to government services, get protection at home and abroad from the government and vote and stand in elections.

Right to citizenship

The question of citizenship starts when we are born. While governments broadly agree on the rights and benefits their citizens should be able to enjoy, different countries have different criteria for acquiring nationality. The Irish government, for example, sets out in its constitution that every person born on Irish territory is automatically an Irish citizen. A person born in Australia, on the other hand, can only become an Australian citizen if at least one parent has Australian citizenship or is legally settled in Australia.

CAZ'S STORY: A MATURE DECISION

Caz's parents moved from Britain to Australia and are legally settled there. This is why Caz could apply for Australian citizenship. She is very proud of her decision to become an Australian citizen.

"When I became an Australian citizen several years ago, I did it for a number of reasons. First of all, I felt stupid not being a naturalised Australian. Having lived here since the age of six, I considered myself to be Australian, and didn't identify as being Scottish, or British – the nationality of my birth. I had to wait till I was over 18 to take out citizenship for myself, because my parents had – and still do have – that apathy towards taking out citizenship that a lot of British immigrants seem to have. For some reason or another it has never seemed all that important to them. But it was important to me. It still is. Pledging my affirmation to Australia is probably one of the most mature things I've ever done."

A Polish man exercises his right as a citizen to vote in his country.

A significant change

For refugees, gaining citizenship in a new country is particularly significant. Refugees from Somalia, for example, fleeing from their own government and country, will remain Somali nationals until they are granted citizenship by another country. If they are successful with their application for citizenship in the new country, they have to give up their Somali nationality. Once this happens, it is very unlikely that the process can be reversed so that they can become nationals of their original country again.

Applying for citizenship

Governments usually have a set of criteria that immigrants must meet to qualify for citizenship. They normally have to show that they can speak the language, have worked or in other ways contributed to society and that they will be responsible citizens. There is no right to citizenship and the authorities can still refuse to grant it if, for example, they decide that the person is not of good character.

AYAAN'S STORY:
BECOMING A DUTCH CITIZEN

Ayaan Hirsi Ali was born in Somalia in 1969. She came to the Netherlands as a refugee in 1992. In September 1997, she became a naturalised Dutch citizen and gave up her Somali nationality. Since January 2003, she has been a member of the lower chamber for the VVD liberal party in the Netherlands. Her decision to take on Dutch nationality was a deliberate one:

"Dual nationality, i.e. Somali and Dutch, was not possible when I decided to become a Dutch national. It was a choice I really needed to think about. But I thought, I'm here now, this is my new homeland and I want to be a true part of this community. From the moment I become a Dutch national I no longer want to act like a foreigner."

Ayaan Hirsi Ali at work in the Dutch parliament.

Changing immigration laws

The immigration agenda

Over the last century, governments in developed countries have increasingly restricted legal immigration. They have revised immigration laws to make it more difficult for people to settle, strengthened controls at ports and airports and tightened rules on who gets a visa and who does not. They have done this to reduce the number of people immigrating from less developed countries, to be seen to be tough on immigration (as they believe this is what the public wants) and in order to try and maintain their own national identity and culture.

Future trends

Developed countries are facing serious challenges. In many, population levels are static or in decline. Some estimate that the population of western Europe could shrink by over 74 million in the next 50 years. People in developed countries are living longer but having fewer children. If these trends continue the numbers of the elderly will begin to outstrip the numbers of young people. This means that, in the future, the working population in developed countries may not be sufficient to keep the economy going.

Workers from abroad

Some argue that the only way to meet this labour shortage is by allowing more people to immigrate. Some countries have already responded by allowing not only highly skilled, but also low- and non-skilled workers from abroad to immigrate. Yet governments are unlikely to change the way they deal with immigration. There is still a reluctance to admit unskilled workers from abroad.

A vicious circle

At the same time, people across less developed and developing countries will continue to want to migrate abroad to improve their standard of living and to find more freedom and safety. But politicians in the developed world do not want to be seen to be encouraging immigration. As a result, more people may decide to immigrate illegally. This, in turn, is only likely to increase the level of hostility that people in developed countries feel towards immigrants. The issue of immigration and the laws connected to it look set to stay on high on governments' agendas for a long time to come.

MEHDI'S STORY: AN UNCERTAIN FUTURE

In 2000, Mehdi Kavousi fled Iran because he feared for his life after taking part in student demonstrations against the Iranian regime. He applied for asylum in the Netherlands, but the authorities rejected his claim and planned to deport him with 23,000 other asylum seekers. To protest against the Dutch government's plans, he sewed his lips together and joined 2,500 others in a demonstration. Alongside him was his Dutch wife, Marjon, whom he met in the Netherlands. Marjon describes his fears:

"Before we went [to the demonstration], he asked me if it was dangerous and whether the police wouldn't round him up. This remark I thought showed how afraid he was."

Even after marriage, Mehdi faces an uncertain future as he does not have the relevant identity papers. Marjon explains:

"In order to get either a visa or passport [for him], we have to go back to Iran. The Dutch authorities maintain that Iran safe is but he knows very well that it is not safe for him and that he will be killed. Yet there is an almost 100% chance that he will have to go back now. We have been living in misery for four years now. We cannot live in uncertainty for one or two years longer."

41

Glossary

act A piece of law passed by a government.

amnesty In the immigration context an amnesty allows a certain group of people who have no or only a temporary immigration status to stay in the country for good.

asylum Special legal immigration status given to people who are recognised as refugees according to the 1951 Refugee Convention.

asylum seeker A person seeking asylum in another country because they fear persecution or danger in their own country.

citizenship If a person has a country's citizenship, it means he or she is a national of that country and holds that country's passport.

constitution A set of values and regulations on which all laws of a country are based.

colony Usually refers to an area of land controlled by a state that is overseas or abroad from it.

deportation The process of forcing a person to leave the country and sending them back – usually to their own country – because they have no valid immigration status.

developed countries High-income countries where people have a high standard of living. These are usually found in Europe and North America, but include Australia, New Zealand and Japan.

developing countries Low- and middle-income countries where people have a lower standard of living and not as many goods and services available to them than in developed countries.

emigrate To leave (go from) your home country to live permanently in another country.

European Union The union of 25 European countries, which works towards shared economic and social goals.

free trade Trade where no tariffs are charged.

human rights A set of rights which everyone in the world should be entitled to, such as the right to free speech, the right to basic education and the right to move freely to other countries.

immigrant A person who has moved permanently to another country to live and work.

immigration laws Laws which set out the circumstances under which people can live and work in a country not their own.

immigration status The kind of permission a person has to stay in another country.

labour exchange An office which helps employers find workers and workers to find employers.

marriage registrar A person employed to perform official marriage ceremonies.

migrant A person going to work in another country usually only for a limited time.

national A person who belongs to a particular nation or state.

passport A document issued by a government to an individual to show that the person is a citizen of that country.

persecution Being punished, tortured or mistreated by a government or a military group, usually because of your political or religious beliefs or ethnic background.

port of entry The various places, such as airports and shipping ports, through which people have to pass to enter a country.

quota A fixed amount – in the immigration context, a quota system means allowing entry to only a fixed number of people from a certain country.

42

Refugee Convention An international law, signed by many countries, that provides safety and protection to refugees arriving in a country.

refugees People living abroad who are recognised under international law as being unable to return to their home country for fear of their lives or loss of freedom.

rights Claims to freedom, equal treatment and resources that are guaranteed by law.

smuggler A person helping another person to travel illegally into another country.

tariffs Taxes charged on imported goods.

trafficker A person who smuggles people abroad and then forces them to work for them against their will.

treaty An official agreement usually between two or more countries.

Ugandan Asians The people and descendants of people who moved from India to Uganda when both countries were still British colonies.

United Nations An international organisation bringing together representatives from 191 countries. The United Nations was set up in 1945 after the Second World War to uphold peace through international co-operation.

visa Official permission from a foreign country to visit it. This is usually given by the country's embassy, who puts a stamp in a person's passport to show that a visa has been granted.

work permit Permission given by immigration authorities in the form of a letter or a stamp in the passport to show that a person is allowed to work in that country.

Yugoslavia A former European country in the Balkans which included the following countries which have become independent or self-ruling: Bosnia-Herzegovina, Croatia, Kosovo, Macedonia, Montenegro, Serbia and Slovenia.

Web connections

International Organisations
International Organisation for Migration (IOM)
www.iom.int

International Labour Organisation (ILO)
www.ilo.org

United Nations (UN)
www.un.org

United Nations High Commissioner for Refugees (UNHCR)
www.unhcr.ch

Non-governmental organisations
Asylumlaw.org
www.asylumlaw.org
Provides information for lawyers on asylum cases.

Australian Refugee Council
www.refugeecouncil.org.au
Supports asylum seekers and refugees in Australia.

British Refugee Council
www.refugeecouncil.org.uk
Supports asylum seekers and refugees in the UK.

Electronic Immigration Network
www.ein.org.uk
On-line gateway to resources on immigration and asylum worldwide.

National Immigration Forum
www.immigrationforum.org
Works to promote the rights of immigrants and refugees in the USA.

US Committee for Refugees and Immigrants
www.refugees.org
US refugee charity.

Government sites
Australian Department of Immigration and Multicultural and Indigenous Affairs
www.immi.gov.au

New Zealand Immigration Service
www.immigration.govt.nz

UK Home Office Immigration and Nationality Directorate
www.ind.homeoffice.gov.uk

Index